What if?

Written by
Kahla Fordyce
Felecia Williams

Edited by
Alisha Adams

Illustrations by
Fuuji Takashi

What if the clouds tasted like cotton candy?

"Yum, the pink clouds taste so good! Which one do you like?" asked Kahla.

"We love them all!" squawked twin Blue Jay birds Jamil and Jamal.

What if rain tasted like sugar?

"My sugar jars are filling up fast," Kahla said. "I can't wait to taste this sugar in Grandma Gwen's sweet pies."

What if the cows can make chocolate milk?

"Mooo. Are you finished, Kahla?" asked Amirah the Cow.

"This chocolate milk is so yummy!" squealed Kahla.

What if mirrors could talk back?

"Good morning, Kahla," said Kahla into the mirror.

"Hey Kahla! What are we wearing today?" asked her reflection.

"Our favorite pink tutu dress! It's picture day today," said Kahla excitedly.

"Make sure we look cute today and don't forget to smile," said her reflection.

"I will," laughed Kahla.

What if the stars sang at night?

"Hmm, hmm, hmm," Kahla hummed with the stars. "La, la, la, I love to dance the night away."

What if winter felt like summer?

"C'mon, Nasir, Let's race," said Kahla.

"Be careful guys, it's slippery out here!" said Aliyah.
"No way, the weather is great!" said Kahla.

What if summer felt like winter?

"It's freezing out here," said Nasir.
"I agree. I miss winter, it's so much fu n,"
said Kahla.
"Stay warm children!"
yelled Grandma Gwen.
"We will," the children replied.
"Hey Aliyah, do you have my gloves?"
asked Kahla.

What if snow tasted like ice cream?

"Vanilla snow ice cream!" yelled the children.

"I think I want to try the chocolate flavor next time," said Amya.

"Yum, yum," said Kahla.

"I am so happy, it's my favorite time of the year!" yelled Derrick.

What if dogs could talk?

"So the park (ruff) was covered in (ruff-ruff) pink slime," said Mrs. Felecia.

"Why was the park covered in pink slime?" asked Kahla.

"(Ruff-ruff) We have to get (ruff-ruff) to the (ruff) end of the book to find out," said Mrs. Felecia.

"Okay, but this basket is getting heavy!" said Greyson.

What if pillows could talk you to sleep?

"Jasmine, you are so comfortable tonight," said Kahla to her pillow. "Good night. I love you."

"I love you too," yawned Jasmine the Pillow. "Sleep well."

What if chairs could hug you?

"I don't know why my cat Andre ran away," said Kahla. "It's getting cold outside. I pray he returns home safe."

"I know Kahla, I know. He will return home soon," hugged Bonnie the Couch.

Just imagine...

www.ingramcontent.com/pod-product-compliance
Lightning Source LLC
Chambersburg PA
CBHW041408160426
42811CB00103B/1552